A Teacher's Guide to *A Christmas Carol*

By Greg Slingerland

A Teacher's Guide to *A Christmas Carol*

First Printing: 2013

ISBN 978-1-300-92459-3

St. Catharines, Ontario, Canada

London during the Life of Dickens

A Christmas Carol was first published on December 19, 1843, in the heart of the Victorian Era. The Victorian Era was a period of time that extended over the reign of Queen Victoria (1837-1901). It was a glorious time for the British Empire – an empire which spanned the globe and on which the 'sun never set'. With this glorious empire came incredible wealth, though only for a portion of the population. A large section of the British people were poor, suffered from malnourishment and were forced to work long hours in difficult conditions. Those who couldn't afford to pay their rents or debt were forced to live in workhouses and debtor prisons. As Charles Dickens famously wrote in *A Tale of Two Cities*, "It was the best of times, it was the worst of times."

Charles Dickens was very concerned about the injustices, poverty and suffering that he saw around him on London streets and society. He had experienced hardship as a child and had to quit school to work in a factory to support his father who had been thrown into a debtors' prison. Dickens believed that the rich, such as Ebenezer Scrooge, had an obligation to help the poor rather than to judge the poor.

Dickens's *A Christmas Carol* struck a note with his readers and transformed the way Christmas was celebrated. More importantly, *A Christmas Carol* highlighted the needs of the poor and destitute in England and around the world. It is a book about compassion and generosity which is why *A Christmas Carol* is a timeless masterpiece that is still enjoyed today.

Chapter 1

Marley's Ghost

1. Who was Marley?

_____

_____

_____

2. Describe Scrooge's character.

_____

_____

_____

_____

3. In what ways are Scrooge and his nephew different?

_____

_____

_____

_____

4. What did Scrooge believe about the poor?

_____

_____

_____

_____

_____

5. What happened when Scrooge came to his front door?

_____

_____

_____

6. Explain this quote: "Darkness is cheap, and Scrooge liked it."

_____

_____

_____

_____

7. How did Scrooge try to convince himself that the ghost of Marley was not real?

_____

_____

_____

_____

_____

8. What was the message of the ghost of Marley? Why was Scrooge being warned?

_____

_____

_____

_____

_____

_____

Define the following words and then use them in a sentence:

Gait

Definition:_____

_____

Sentence: _____

_____

Trifle

Definition:_____

_____

Sentence: _____

_____

Palpable

Definition:_____

_____

Sentence: _____

_____

Impropriety

Definition:_____

_____

Sentence: _____

_____

Kindred

Definition:_____

_____

Sentence: _____

_____

Pageant

Definition:_____

_____

Sentence: _____

_____

Spectre

Definition:_____

_____

Sentence: _____

_____

Fatigue

Definition:_____

_____

Sentence: _____

_____

Write a Christmas Carol Haiku!

A haiku is a short poem that uses sensory language to show feeling or to portray an image. Haikus are usually made up of three lines. The first line has five syllables, the second line seven syllables, and the third line has five syllables.

> Over the wintry
> forest, winds howl in rage
> with no leaves to blow.
>
> - *Natsume Soseki*

Write a haiku reflecting the desolate mood of chapter one in the box below. Illustrate the border with scenes from the chapter.

Chapter 1 - Answers

Marley's Ghost

1. Who was Marley?

Charles Dickens begins his book by making the case that Marley is dead, though Scrooge doesn't seem to be upset by Marely's demise. Old Marley, or Jacob Marley, was Ebenezer Scrooge's old business partner. They were kindred spirits in that they were both ruthless and heartless businessmen. They both took pleasure in their bankbooks and not in each other's company. Marley dies without anyone mourning his loss – including Scrooge, who hasn't even bothered to take Marley's name off of the door. It doesn't concern Scrooge when clients mistakenly refer to Scrooge as Marley.

2. Describe Scrooge's character.

"Oh! But he was a tight-fisted hand at the grindstone, Scrooge! A squeezing, wrenching, grasping, scraping, clutching, covetous old sinner! Hard and sharp as flint, from which no steel had ever struck out generous fire; secret, and self-contained, and solitary as an oyster. The cold within him froze his old features, nipped his pointed nose, shrivelled his cheek, stiffened his gait; made his eyes red, his thin lips blue; and spoke out shrewdly in his grating voice… He carried his own low temperature always about with him; he iced his office in the dog-days; and didn't thaw it one degree at Christmas."

Scrooge was disliked by all who came into contact with and many avoided Scrooge. Dickens points out that even "the blindmen's dogs appeared to know him; and when they saw him coming on, would tug their owners into doorways and up courts…" Scrooge though didn't care and liked to be left alone. Money was his idol, religion and his master. Above all, Scrooge detests the Christmas season and the good-tidings that come with the season.

3. In what ways are Scrooge and his nephew different?

Scrooge's nephew Fred has a zest for life and takes an active interest in those around him. He continues to reach out to his embittered Uncle Ebenezer despite Scrooge's protests and scorn. Fred welcomes the Christmas season and the spirit of generosity that comes with this holiday while his uncle reacts fiercely to Christmas goodwill. Fred has not been possessed by the pursuit of riches and is quite content with his life. Scrooge looks down on his nephew for not using his talents properly and for wasting his time and money on Christmas. Fred makes an impassioned speech to his uncle about how Christmas has done him good and how it is a time for charity and renewal. Scrooge declares 'humbug' and then to prove his point further, chases out two gentlemen who were seeking alms for the poor.

4. What did Scrooge believe about the poor?

Scrooge believes that the poor have nothing to be happy about and have no reason to be celebrating Christmas. He criticizes his own employee (who Scrooge himself poorly pays) for celebrating Christmas. "...my clerk, with fifteen shillings a week, and a wife and family, talking about a merry Christmas. I'll retire to an asylum."

When the two gentlemen ask Scrooge for a Christmas donation to relieve the poor, Scrooge responds that the workhouses and prisons are there for the poor. When told that many of the poor would rather die than be subjected to a poor-prison or workhouse Scrooge coldly responds "If they would rather die they had better do it, and decrease the surplus population."

5. What happened when Scrooge came to his front door?

Scrooge had quite forgotten about that afternoon's mention of Marley and the fact that Marley had died seven years ago to the day. Yet, when Scrooge put the key into the lock, the knocker changed into the face of Marley. It was a horrible sight to Scrooge and the image was incredibly life-like. "It was not angry or ferocious, but looked at Scrooge as Marley used to look: with ghostly spectacles turned up upon its ghostly forehead."

6. Explain this quote: "Darkness is cheap, and Scrooge liked it."

Scrooge loved the darkness for economic reasons – it reminded him that he was saving money by not lighting up his house. Since Scrooge was only focussed on his accounts and business transactions, nothing else mattered to him or even bothered him. This quote also alludes to the gospel of John 3:19 where Jesus says "And this is the condemnation, that the light has come into the world, and men loved darkness rather than light, because their deeds were evil. For everyone practicing evil hates the light and does not come to the light, lest his deeds should be exposed."

7. How did Scrooge try to convince himself that the ghost of Marley was not real?

Scrooge is a rational person who deals with number all day. He studies his ledgers and accounts to make sure everything adds up. He can't accept this irrational presence of Jacob Marely who has been dead for seven years. The ghost of Marley asks Scrooge why he doesn't believe and he responds that the sense are easily affected. "A slight disorder of the stomach makes them cheat. You may be an undigested bit of beef, a blot of mustard, a crumb of cheese, a fragment of an underdone potato. There's more of gravy than of grave about you, whatever you are!" Scrooge then tries to rationalize the appearance by saying that by swallowing a toothpick he could just as easily conjure up legions of goblins that would bother him for the rest of his days.

8. What was the message of the ghost of Marley? Why was Scrooge being warned?

Marley tells Scrooge that the chains he wears were forged by his deeds and actions. Marley made each link by his own free will. Now he is doomed to wander the earth while being fettered and weighed down. Marley warns Scrooge that though he couldn't see or feel chains, Scrooge was no different than Marley and should be prepared for the same doom.

Scrooge lauds Marley for being a good man of business but Marley angrily responds "Business! Mankind was my business. The common welfare was my business; charity, mercy, forbearance, and benevolence, were all my business. The dealings of my trade were but a drop of water in the comprehensive ocean of my business!"

Marley laments that he had his eyes cast turned down (or focussed on himself). "Why did I walk through crowds of fellow-beings with my eyes turned down, and never raise them to that blessed Star which led the Wise Men to a poor abode? Were there no poor homes to which its light would have conducted me!"

Scrooge was being warned by Marley not to tread the same path or to suffer the same fate. Marley is telling Scrooge to accept the advice of the three ghosts that were to visit him and to lift up his eyes to his fellow man.

Chapter 2

The First of the Three Spirits

1. Describe in the detail the visitor that appeared at Scrooge's bedside.

_____

_____

_____

_____

_____

2. Where did the Ghost first take Scrooge?

_____

_____

_____

3. Why didn't the people Scrooge and the Ghost were watching notice their presence?

_____

_____

_____

4. Why did Scrooge weep when he saw himself as a young boy?

_____

_____

_____

5. Scrooge's heart is pricked when he sees himself as a little boy. What does this sight make him wish he could change from his actions from the previous day?

_____

_____

_____

_____

6. What became of Scrooge's sister? What did she leave behind?

_____

_____

_____

7. What impact did the sight and flood of memories of Fezziwig have on Scrooge? What did these happy memories make Scrooge regret?

_____
_____
_____
_____
_____

8. Why did Belle break off the engagement between herself and Scrooge?

_____
_____
_____

9. Describe the last scene that the Ghost showed Scrooge. What was similar about the first and the last scene?

_____
_____
_____
_____
_____
_____

Define the following words and then use them in a sentence:

Opaque

Definition:_____
_____

Sentence: _____
_____

Jocund

Definition:_____
_____

Sentence: _____
_____

Melancholy

Definition:_____
_____

Sentence: _____
_____

Past Memories...

Name: _____

Scrooge had both pleasant memories and sad memories of his past. Scrooge was at some points filled with joy and anguish at reliving his past. Re-examining his past also motivated Scrooge to change his ways. Memories are powerful agents that can be triggered by pictures, stories, music, or even smells. Imagine how dull life would be without memories – they remind us of the good and the bad times; they change us and they bond people together. We learn from our memories, and we treasure certain memories.

Write about a memory that sticks out in your mind. What prompts this memory? Is it a smell, a sound, a person, a picture, or something else? Is it a pleasant memory or a painful memory? How has this memory changed you?

_____

_____

_____

_____

_____

_____

_____

_____

_____

_____

_____

_____

_____

_____

_____

_____

_____

_____

_____

_____

Chapter 2 - Answers

The First of the Three Spirits

1. Describe in the detail the visitor that appeared at Scrooge's bedside.

The visitor that appears at Scrooge's bedside is the Ghost of Christmas Past. The purpose of this spectre is to show Scrooge his past through various tableaus.

"It was a strange figure – like a child: yet not so like a child as like an old man, viewed through some supernatural medium, which gave him the appearance of having receded from the view, and being diminished to a child's proportions. Its hair, which hung about its neck and down its back, was white as if with age; and yet the face had not a wrinkle in it, and the tenderest bloom was on the skin. The arms were very long and muscular; the hands the same, as if its hold were of uncommon strength. Its legs and feet, most delicately formed, were, like those upper members, bare. It wore a tunic of the purest white and round its waist was bound a lustrous belt, the sheen of which was beautiful. It held a fresh green holly in its hand; and, in contradiction of that wintry emblem, had its dress trimmed with summer flowers. But the strangest thing about it was, that from the crown of its head there sprung a bright clear jet of light, by which all things was visible…"

2. Where did the Ghost first take Scrooge?

The Ghost took Scrooge to where he grew up as a boy. It was a place that Scrooge had fond memories of and was quickly caught up in all of the familiar sights. Scrooge's mood was dampened however by the melancholy sight of a lonely book sitting by himself in the back of a house. Scrooge recognizes this boy to be himself and weeps at the pain of those lonesome moments. Though Scrooge was "hard and sharp as flint" he cries out "poor boy!" in pity at the sight of himself.

3. Why didn't the people Scrooge and the Ghost were watching notice their presence?

Scrooge and the Ghost did not actually go back in time but were merely looking at "shadows of the things that have been". The Ghost was in essence jogging Scrooge's memories that Scrooge had buried away.

4. Why did Scrooge weep when he saw himself as a young boy?

Scrooge suddenly remembered the pain and anguish of being alone as a child and spending Christmas away from his family. He cried out because of the lonely memories, from the pain of having an angry father and from being separated from his family and friends.

5. Scrooge's heart is pricked when he sees himself as a little boy. What does this sight make him wish he could change from his actions from the previous day?

Scrooge remembers the boy that had come to his door that night offering to sing a carol in return for a donation. Scrooge had chased him off his doorstep in anger. He now felt pity for the boy after remembering his own hurt as a boy, and wishes he could give the boy some money.

6. What became of Scrooge's sister? What did she leave behind?

Scrooge loved his sister and rejoiced with her that their father had changed for the better. Little Fan was "a delicate creature...but she had a large heart." Little Fan died (presumably while giving birth to her son). She died leaving behind her son, Scrooge's nephew, Fred.

7. What impact did the sight and flood of memories of Fezziwig have on Scrooge? What did these happy memories make Scrooge regret?

Scrooge is flooded with happy memories of his time with Fezziwig. The Ghost brings him to the scene of one of the many festive Christmas parties that Old Fezziwig and Mrs. Fezziwig threw each year. "During the whole of this time, Scrooge had acted like a man out of his wits. His heart and soul were in the scene, and with his former self..."

The differences between Fezziwig of the past and Scrooge of the present are stark. Scrooge begrudges his employee for wanting time off for Christmas and then insists that he come in all the earlier the following morning. Fezziwig clears away all of the office furniture, brings in fine foods and musicians and enjoys spending time with his employees and family. Fezziwig had the "fuel heaped upon the fire" whereas Scrooge's fire in his office was a mere spark that his employee Bob Cratchit extinguished by trying to stoke the flame.

Scrooge realizes that and employer "has the power to render us happy or unhappy; to make our service light or burdensome; a pleasure or a toil..." He regrets that he did not treat his clerk, Bob Cratchit, better. He wanted to say some kind words to his clerk.

8. Why did Belle break off the engagement between herself and Scrooge?

Belle comes to the sad realization that the years of business have changed Scrooge. Scrooge's priorities have changed and is now intent on making money. Belle tells Scrooge that an idol has displaced her – "a golden one". She explains to Scrooge "I have seen your nobler aspirations fall off one by one, until the master-passion, Gain, engrosses you." Belle finalizes her case with the argument that had Scrooge came across her at the present point in time, Scrooge would never engage himself to a dowerless girl with such little prospects.

9. Describe the last scene that the Ghost showed Scrooge. What was similar about the first and the last scene?

The last scene that the Ghost shows Scrooge also involves Belle, but years later. Belle has a family of her own – a large family – and seems to be incandescently happy. Belle's house is filled with joy and contentment. After all the family's excitement has died down, Belle and her husband settle down by the fire where Belle's husband informs her that he has seen an old acquaintance of Belle – Mr. Scrooge.

As in the first scene, Scrooge is alone. The husband reports that Scrooge was "Quite alone in the world, I do believe." Scrooge, who is watching these scenes pass by, is once again saddened by the loneliness and lack of joy in his life.

Chapter 3

The Second of the Three Spirits

1. Who was the second ghost that visited Scrooge? What did he look like?

_____

_____

_____

_____

2. How has Scrooge's attitude changed towards the visits by the three spirits?

_____

_____

_____

_____

3. Who is Tiny Tim? What do we all learn about him in this chapter?

_____

_____

_____

_____

_____

4. Why does Tiny Tim hope people saw him in the church?

_____

_____

_____

_____

_____

5. What does the Ghost mean when he says "I see a vacant seat in the poor chimney corner, and a crutch without an owner, carefully preserved. If these shadows remain unaltered by the Future, the child will die."?

_____

_____

_____

_____

6. What words spoken by Scrooge earlier (and now quoted by the Ghost) to the two men collecting money for the poor does Scrooge now repent of?

_____

_____

_____

_____

_____

7. Explain this quote from the Ghost: "_Will you decide what men shall live, what men shall die? It may be, that in the sight of Heaven, you are more worthless and less fit to live than millions like this poor man's child._"

_____

_____

_____

_____

_____

8. How did Scrooge become the punch-line of the _Yes and No_ game at Scrooge's nephew's house?

_____

_____

_____

_____

9. What impact did the Ghost have on all the places far and near he visited and the people he passed by?

_____

_____

_____

_____

10. What surprising transformation happens with the Ghost? What is the Ghost's explanation?

_____

_____

_____

_____

_____

11. What do the two children symbolize who are crouched down at the feet of Ghost?

_____

_____

_____

_____

Define the following words and then use them in a sentence:

Spectre

Definition:_____

_____

Sentence: _____

_____

Capacious

Definition:_____

_____

Sentence: _____

_____

Descriptions in *A Christmas Carol*

Charles Dickens painted elaborate pictures through his descriptions in the third chapter. He hits all of our senses when describing the sights, smell, and sounds of the different scenes Scrooge is shown.

Choose one of the following scenes: Scrooge's transformed room at the beginning of the chapter, the Ghost of Christmas Present, or the scene on the street outside. Illustrate the scene in the box below using the detailed descriptions. Include as many details as possible.

Irony in *A Christmas Carol*

Irony is used in literature to add drama, excitement or humour to a story. *A Christmas Carol* makes use of irony on many occasions and keeps the reader interested. A basic definition of irony is when the unexpected happens instead of the expected. Simple examples could be "The fire hall burned down" or "The meeting for procrastinators has been postponed". In *A Christmas Carol*, Scrooge's words come back to haunt him. When he asks about what the fate of Tiny Tim will be and whether he will be spared or not, the Ghost dredges up Scrooge's former condemning words: "*If he be like to die, he had better do it, and decrease the surplus situation.*"

Write a short story about a contest with an ironic ending.

Chapter 3 - Answers

The Second of the Three Spirits

1. Who was the second ghost that visited Scrooge? What did he look like?

The second ghost that visited Scrooge was the Ghost of Christmas Present. The Ghost was wearing a simple green robe which was edged with white fur. The robe hung loosely and showed the bare chest of the Ghost. The Ghost had bare feet and a holly wreath sat atop a head of long brown curly hair. The Ghost had sparkling eyes, a cheery voice and a joyful air. The Ghost has a big heart and the open robe symbolizes an open heart. He also has an empty scabbard which symbolizes peace and the celebration of the 'Prince of Peace'.

2. How has Scrooge's attitude changed towards the visits by the three spirits?

Scrooge is open to change and states "Spirit, conduct me where you will. I went forth last night on compulsion, and I learnt a lesson which is working now. Tonight, if you have to teach me, let me profit by it."

3. Who is Tiny Tim? What do we all learn about him in this chapter?

Tiny Tim is Bob Cratchit's crippled son. Tiny Tim is not healthy though Bob unconvincingly tries to tell his family that Tim is growing strong and healthy. Bob is very close to Tim and dreads the thought that Tim might die in his childhood. The Ghost tells Scrooge that unless things change, the child will die.

4. Why does Tiny Tim hope people saw him in the church?

Tiny Tim hopes people saw him in the church because then they would be reminded about the true message of Christmas – that Jesus was born and came to the world to save people in need. "…he hoped the people saw him in the church, because he was a cripple, and it might be pleasant to them to remember upon Christmas Day, who made lame beggars walk, and blind men see."

5. What does the Ghost mean when he says "I see a vacant seat in the poor chimney corner, and a crutch without an owner, carefully preserved. If these shadows remain unaltered by the Future, the child will die."?

The Ghost is telling Scrooge that unless the Cratchit's situation changes, Tiny Tim will die. Scrooge is being told that he would be responsible for this because of his coldness and lack of care. Scrooge scorns Bob for his meagre salary and yet it is Scrooge who pays Bob Cratchit. Scrooge has condemned the Cratchit family to a life of poverty and destitution.

6. What words spoken by Scrooge earlier (and now quoted by the Ghost) to the two men collecting money for the poor does Scrooge now repent of?

"What then? If he be like to die, he had better do it, and decrease the surplus population."

7. Explain this quote from the Ghost: *"Will you decide what men shall live, what men shall die? It may be, that in the sight of Heaven, you are more worthless and less fit to live than millions like this poor man's child."*

The Ghost rebukes Scrooge for being so heartless and for ruling that the poor have no purpose and reason to continue living. Scrooge defined purpose and worth based on one's material worth. The Ghost points out that in the grand scheme of things, in the sight of Heaven, money has no value and Scrooge may be more worthless than even the poorest child.

8. How did Scrooge become the punch-line of the *Yes and No* game at Scrooge's nephew's house?

The game is played by players asking a serious of questions to which the leader of the game can only answer yes and no. The players take turns asking questions hoping to reveal the word that the leader of the game is thinking of. In the game played by Fred and his friends, Fred laughs at the irony of some of the questions. Fred answers yes to the questions asking if the word in question is a disagreeable, savage, and grunting animal that prowls the streets of London. When the 'plump sister' finally solves the riddle of the animal being Uncle Scrooge, the room dissolves into uproarious laughter.

9. What impact did the Ghost have on all the places far and near he visited and the people he passed by?

The Ghost brought Scrooge to many places and each visit had a happy end. "The Spirit stood beside sick beds, and they were cheerful; on foreign lands, and they were close at home; by struggling men, and they were patient in their greater hope; by every refuge, where man in his little brief life had not locked the door and barred the Spirit out, he left his blessing, and taught Scrooge his truths."

10. What surprising transformation happens with the Ghost? What is the Ghost's explanation?

After a long night of visiting different places, Scrooge notices that the Ghost is noticeably older. The Ghost's hair turns grey. The Ghost explains that his life in this world is very short and that it would end that very night.

11. What do the two children symbolize who are crouched down at the feet of Ghost?

The two children symbolize 'ignorance' and 'want'. The children do not belong to the Ghost but belong to man. Man's ignorance of the downtrodden and the lowly and man's lack of charity have left these children in this sickly state. Scrooge had been ignorant of the great needs around him – he had shut the messengers of truth out. He ignored his nephew, didn't know anything about Bob Cratchit and his family, chased the caroler away, and lambasted the men seeking alms for trying to help the poor. Because of his willful ignorance, many around Scrooge needlessly suffered. Scrooge shows his ignorance when he asks if there is any help for these children. The Ghost sharply rebuts with a quote from Scrooge himself: "Are there no prisons? Are there no workhouses?"

Chapter 4

The Last of the Three Spirits

1. Describe the third ghost. Who was he?

_____

_____

_____

_____

2. The Ghost does not speak to Scrooge, is always leading Scrooge forward, and has his hand pointed straight ahead. What does the Ghost of Christmas Yet to Come symbolize?

_____

_____

_____

_____

3. Irony can occur when the readers knows something that the main character does not. What is the irony in this chapter?

_____

_____

_____

_____

4. Who is 'Old Scratch'?

_____

5. What was the connection between Old Joe and Scrooge?

_____

_____

_____

_____

6. When Scrooge asks the Ghost to "show him someone who feels emotion caused by this man's death", who does the Ghost show to Scrooge? What kind of emotion do they feel and why?

_____

_____

_____

_____

_____

7. What event has impacted the Cratchit family? Describe the scene in detail.

_____

_____

_____

_____

_____

8. Scrooge is brought before a tombstone. Before looking at the name engraved on the stone, Scrooge asks the Ghost "Answer me one question. Are these the shadows of the things that Will be, or are they shadows of things that May be, only?" What was Scrooge asking?

_____

_____

_____

_____

_____

9. What connection can you make between the story of Jacob wrestling with the angel in Genesis 32 and Scrooge's pleading with the Ghost?

_____

_____

_____

_____

Symbols in *A Christmas Carol*

Dickens uses many symbols throughout A Christmas Carol. Symbolism occurs when an abstract object or person comes to represent a person, thing, or idea. An example of a symbol would be a *maple leaf* which is a symbolic representation of *Canada*.

Listed below are some of the symbols found *A Christmas Carol*. Think carefully about each symbol and explain what these symbols mean or represent.

Symbol	Meaning
Marley's Chains	
Scrooge's Gravestone	
Scrooge's Bed	
Fezziwig	
Fan	
Tiny Tim	
Cold and Foggy Weather	
Two Men Collecting Alms	
Cratchit Feast	
Spirit's Open Robe	
Scrooge's Cold Office	
There are many more symbols in A Christmas Carol. Find two more and explain their meanings.	

Symbols in *A Christmas Carol* - Answers

Dickens uses many symbols throughout A Christmas Carol. Symbolism occurs when an abstract object or person comes to represent a person, thing, or idea. An example of a symbol would be a *maple leaf* which is a symbolic representation of *Canada*.

Listed below are some of the symbols found *A Christmas Carol*. Think carefully about each symbol and explain what these symbols mean or represent.

Symbol	Meaning
Marley's Chains	The chains represent greed. Marley forged the chains himself through his own greed. The clanging chains are a constant reminder to him.
Scrooge's Gravestone	Scrooge's impending death. The gravestone appears to be in a forgotten and neglected cemetery.
Scrooge's Bed	Scrooge's private sanctuary. It is repeatedly referred in the story. The ghosts invade his curtained bed. At the end, the bed is normal again.
Fezziwig	Generosity, Christmas cheer, goodwill and goodwill. He represents what every good employer should be like.
Fan	Family and caring. Family relationships and restoration.
Tiny Tim	Innocence. Christmas blessing. What Jesus Christ calls us to be like – little children.
Cold and Foggy Weather	Scrooge's heart at the beginning of the story.
Two Men Collecting Alms	Charity
Cratchit Feast	Even in the midst of want and need, the Cratchits are still able to enjoy a Christmas feast. One doesn't need to be wealthy for Christmas.
Spirit's Open Robe	The Ghost is inviting and caring. His big heart is open to all who haven't shut out the spirit.
Scrooge's Cold Office	Scrooge's way of doing business. He didn't care how coldly he treated people or how he treated his employees.

There are many more symbols in A Christmas Carol. Find two more and explain their meanings.

Chapter 4 - Answers

The Last of the Three Spirits

1. Describe the third ghost. Who was he?

The third ghost was the Ghost of Christmas Yet to Come. He was a "solemn phantom, draped and hooded, coming, like a mist along the ground..." He had the appearance and symbolism of the Grim Reaper. "It was shrouded in a deep black garment, which concealed its head, its face, its form, and left nothing of it visible save one outstretched hand."

2. The Ghost does not speak to Scrooge, is always leading Scrooge forward, and has his hand pointed straight ahead. What does the Ghost of Christmas Yet to Come symbolize?

The Ghost Yet to Come symbolizes death – inevitable death. It doesn't talk, but it is always proceeding and always pointing. The tableau's that are shown in this chapter are about death and death's relentless march. Time is constantly on the move and does not wait. "Therefore never send to know for whom the bells tolls; it tolls for thee."

3. Irony can occur when the readers knows something that the main character does not. What is the irony in this chapter?

Scrooge does not realize that the people in this chapter are referring to him as the person who has passed away. Though Scrooge does suspect it towards the end, his fears and suspicions are not confirmed until he sees his name carved in the cold stone of the gravestone.

4. Who is 'Old Scratch'?

Old Scratch is the devil. The men talking about Scrooge have no doubt that the devil has claimed Scrooge.

5. What was the connection between old Joe and Scrooge?

Old Joe is a pawnbroker and is making deals with various customers who are trying to pawn some of Scrooge's remaining possessions. Scrooge's charwoman (cleaner) and laundress have arrived, as has the undertaker. They have taken things from Scrooge's home and person. They are happy to be making a quick buck off of Scrooge.

6. When Scrooge asks the Ghost to "show him someone who feels emotion caused by this man's death", who does the Ghost show to Scrooge? What kind of emotion do they feel and why?

The Ghost brings Scrooge to the house of a young couple. They are tired and worn but have cause to celebrate at the news that their creditor (Scrooge) is dying. His death will bring them some extra time to come up with their next payment.

7. What event has impacted the Cratchit family? Describe the scene.

Tiny Tim has died and the whole family is feeling his loss deeply. The joy that the Cratchit's had formerly enjoyed has evaporated and has been replaced by a heavy feeling of grief. Scrooge finds Mrs. Cratchit and her daughters busily sewing – presumably black mourning clothes. The previous spirit had predicted an empty chair and now Scrooge is show Bob grieving before Tiny Tim's little chair that is now vacant. The Ghost tells Scrooge that Tiny Tim had a childish essence from God. This is an allusion to Christ's valuing of children. Dickens is pointing out that children are too often overlooked by society – especially children like Tiny Tim who often seen as a hindrance instead of a blessing.

8. Scrooge is brought before a tombstone. Before looking at the name engraved on the stone, Scrooge asks the Ghost "Answer me one question. Are these the shadows of the things that Will be, or are they shadows of things that May be, only?" What was Scrooge asking?

Scrooge wants to know if he can change his fate. He recognizes the wretchedness of his existence and vows to change.

9. What connection can you make between the story of Jacob wrestling with the angel in Genesis 32 and Scrooge's pleading with the Ghost?

Jacob struggles vainly against a stranger in Genesis 32. Jacob realizes that the stranger is an angel – a messenger. He won't stop wrestling with the angel until he receives a blessing. Jacob can't prevail against the angel, but the angel does bless Jacob. Jacob's name is changed to Israel. Like Jacob, Scrooge wrestles with the Ghost. He refuses to accept a miserable fate after realizing his selfish folly. He pleads with the Ghost and finally tries to arrest the hand that symbolizes the inevitable advance of life into death. The Ghost, like the angel is stronger and is not repulsed by Scrooge. Scrooge prays for mercy and the Ghost turns into his bedpost. Like Jacob, Scrooge is forever changed by this encounter and knows that his life will never be the same again.

Chapter 5

The End of It

1. What is different about Scrooge's character in this last chapter? Be specific.

   _____

   _____

   _____

   _____

   _____

2. When Scrooge meets the man who was collecting donations for the poor (from chapter 1), what is Scrooge's response?

   _____

   _____

   _____

3. As Scrooge walks through the streets, how does he show that he is different in both word and deed?

   _____

   _____

   _____

   _____

4. How does Scrooge make amends, or make things right, with Bob Cratchit?

   _____

   _____

   _____

5. How does one keep Christmas every day?

   _____

   _____

   _____

Writing an Epilogue...

An epilogue is "a concluding part added to a literary work." *A Christmas Carol* does not have an epilogue which means that Dickens's readers are left to their own imaginations as to how Scrooge lives out the rest of his days. We know that Ebenezer Scrooge is a changed man and has vowed to live every day with Christmas in his heart, but we don't know *how* he does that.

Write an epilogue for *A Christmas Carol*. In your epilogue, inform your readers about how Scrooge shows his newfound generosity, what happens to Tiny Tim, Bob Cratchit, and his nephew Fred. Be creative and keep your epilogue true to the ending of *A Christmas Carol*.

_____

_____

_____

_____

_____

_____

_____

_____

_____

_____

_____

_____

_____

_____

_____

_____

_____

_____

_____

_____

_____

_____

Chapter 5 - Answers

The End of It

1. What is different about Scrooge's character in this last chapter? Be specific.

Scrooge's entire outlook on life is different – he is a new man. He makes a vow to live differently to old Jacob. His emotions are different as well. The old Scrooge was miserable and angry whereas the new Scrooge is laughing and crying. Joy courses through him. Dickens also points out that he has an 'illustrative' laugh. Scrooge didn't even crack a smile before. Scrooge also says at one point that he is "quite a baby" – this is an allusion to Christ saying that only those who are born again will enter the Kingdom of Heaven. Scrooge notices the peal of bells and is excited by the tidings that the church bells bring.

2. When Scrooge meets the man who was collecting donations for the poor (from chapter 1), what is Scrooge's response?

Scrooge knew that he cause the man pain and anger and was determined to right this wrong when he saw the man out on the street. Scrooge wishes the man a merry Christmas and then donates an amount that makes up for the many years of stinginess. "A great many back-payments are included in it, I assure you." This is part of the vow of living in the spirit of Christmas past. Not only does Scrooge want to live better, but he wants to make amends.

3. As Scrooge walks through the streets, how does he show that he is different in both word and deed?

Scrooge "went to church, and walked about the streets, and watched the people hurrying to and fro, and patted children on the head, and questioned beggars, and looked down into the kitchens of houses…" Scrooge is taking example from the Ghost of Christmas Present who was a blessing to whomever he passed. Scrooge also visits with his nephew Fred.

4. How does Scrooge make amends, or make things right, with Bob Cratchit?

Scrooge buys the big turkey that is in the store window and plans to give it to the Cratchits. He also raises Bob's salary, and assists his struggling family. Life in the office is different now as well. Scrooge and Bob talk over a bowl of soup and allows Bob to put more coal on the fire. "To Tiny Tim, he was a second father."

5. How does one keep Christmas every day?

Scrooge's newfound generosity was not fleeting, nor did it end at Christmas. Scrooge continued to live every day as if it was Christmas. He had a spirit of joy and generosity and sought to lift his fellow man up as if it was Christmas day. Christmas is a time to remember the birth of Christ – the person who, in the words of Tiny Tim, "made lame beggars walk, and blind men see." Just as Christ selflessly gave of himself and helped his fellow man (to the point of death on the cross) so to should everyone give selflessly – not just on the birthday of Christ, but every day.

A Christmas Carol – Final Test

/30   Name: _____

<u>Multiple Choice</u>: Circle the correct letter. (5)

1. What city does *A Christmas Carol* take place in?

    a. Paris

    b. London

    c. Manchester

    d. Toronto

2. Scrooge exclaimed this word whenever he thought something was nonsense:

    a. Snapperdoodle

    b. Humdinger

    c. Falalalala

    d. Humbug

3. Scrooge's doorknocker changed to this:

    a. The face of his old business partner Marley

    b. The face of the Ghost of Christmas Past

    c. The face of Tiny Tim

    d. The face of a poor child

4. The name of Scrooge's sister:

    a. Big Bertha

    b. Mini Lu

    c. Small Suzy

    d. Little Fan

5. Scrooge's first employer was:

    a. Marley

    b. Cratchit

    c. Fezziwig

    d. Dickens

Short Answers: Answer the following questions in complete sentences. All questions are worth one point unless otherwise noted. (12)

1. What did Scrooge believe about the poor?

_____

_____

_____

_____

_____

2. What was the message of the ghost of Marley? Why was Scrooge being warned? (2)

_____

_____

_____

_____

_____

_____

3. Why did Belle break off the engagement between herself and Scrooge?

_____

_____

_____

_____

4. Who was the second ghost that visited Scrooge? What did he look like? (2)

_____

_____

_____

_____

_____

5. Who is Tiny Tim? Provide two details. (2)

_____

_____

_____

_____

_____

6. Describe the third ghost. Who was he? (2)

_____

_____

_____

_____

7. How does Scrooge make amends, or make things right, with Bob Cratchit? (2)

_____

_____

_____

_____

Paragraph Answers. Answer the following questions in a proper paragraph. (13)

1. What does the Ghost mean when he says "I see a vacant seat in the poor chimney corner, and a crutch without an owner, carefully preserved. If these shadows remain unaltered by the Future, the child will die."? (4)

_____

_____

_____

_____

_____

_____

_____

_____

2. The Ghost of Christmas Yet to Come does not speak to Scrooge, is always leading Scrooge forward, and has his hand pointed straight ahead. What does the Ghost of Christmas Yet to Come symbolize? Carefully explain. (4)

_____

_____

_____

_____

_____

_____

_____

_____

_____

3. After reading *A Christmas Carol* what do you think Dickens thinks about wealth and money? Does Dickens think wealth breeds greed or is he saying something altogether different? Explain and use examples to back up your argument. (5)

_____

_____

_____

_____

_____

_____

_____

_____

_____

_____

_____

_____

Bonus: Who is old Scratch? _____

A Christmas Carol – Final Test – <u>Answer Key</u>

/30   Name: <u>Key</u>

<u>Multiple Choice</u>: Circle the correct letter. (5)

1. What city does *A Christmas Carol* take place in?

   e. Paris

   f. <u>London</u>

   g. Manchester

   h. Toronto

2. Scrooge exclaimed this word whenever he thought something was nonsense:

   a. Snapperdoodle

   b. Humdinger

   c. Falalalala

   d. <u>Humbug</u>

3. Scrooge's doorknocker changed to this:

   a. <u>The face of his old business partner Marley</u>

   b. The face of the Ghost of Christmas Past

   c. The face of Tiny Tim

   d. The face of a poor child

4. The name of Scrooge's sister:

   a. Big Bertha

   b. Mini Lu

   c. Small Suzy

   d. <u>Little Fan</u>

5. Scrooge's first employer was:

   a. Marley

   b. Cratchit

   c. <u>Fezziwig</u>

   d. Dickens

<u>Short Answers</u>: Answer the following questions in complete sentences. All questions are worth one point unless otherwise noted. (12)

1. What did Scrooge believe about the poor?

Scrooge believes that the poor have nothing to be happy about and have no reason to be celebrating Christmas. He criticizes his own employee (who Scrooge himself poorly pays) for celebrating Christmas. "...my clerk, with fifteen shillings a week, and a wife and family, talking about a merry Christmas. I'll retire to an asylum."

When the two gentlemen ask Scrooge for a Christmas donation to relieve the poor, Scrooge responds that the workhouses and prisons are there for the poor. When told that many of the poor would rather die than be subjected to a poor-prison or workhouse Scrooge coldly responds "If they would rather die they had better do it, and decrease the surplus population."

2. What was the message of the ghost of Marley? Why was Scrooge being warned? (2)

Marley tells Scrooge that the chains he wears were forged by his deeds and actions. Marley made each link by his own free will. Now he is doomed to wander the earth while being fettered and weighed down. Marley warns Scrooge that though he couldn't see or feel chains, Scrooge was no different than Marley and should be prepared for the same doom.

Scrooge lauds Marley for being a good man of business but Marley angrily responds "Business! Mankind was my business. The common welfare was my business; charity, mercy, forbearance, and benevolence, were all my business. The dealings of my trade were but a drop of water in the comprehensive ocean of my business!"

Marley laments that he had his eyes cast turned down (or focussed on himself). "Why did I walk through crowds of fellow-beings with my eyes turned down, and never raise them to that blessed Star which led the Wise Men to a poor abode? Were there no poor homes to which its light would have conducted me!"

Scrooge was being warned by Marley not to tread the same path or to suffer the same fate. Marley is telling Scrooge to accept the advice of the three ghosts that were to visit him and to lift up his eyes to his fellow man.

3. Why did Belle break off the engagement between herself and Scrooge?

Belle comes to the sad realization that the years of business have changed Scrooge. Scrooge's priorities have changed and is now intent on making money. Belle tells Scrooge that an idol has displaced her — "a golden one". She explains to Scrooge "I have seen your nobler aspirations fall off one by one, until the master-passion, Gain, engrosses you."

Belle finalizes her case with the argument that had Scrooge came across her at the present point in time, Scrooge would never engage himself to a dowerless girl with such little prospects.

4. Who was the second ghost that visited Scrooge? What did he look like? (2)

The second ghost that visited Scrooge was the Ghost of Christmas Present. The Ghost was wearing a simple green robe which was edged with white fur. The robe hung loosely and showed the bare chest of the Ghost. The Ghost had bare feet and a holly wreath sat atop a head of long brown curly hair. The Ghost had sparkling eyes, a cheery voice and a joyful air. The Ghost has a big heart and the open robe symbolizes an open heart. He also has an empty scabbard which symbolizes peace and the celebration of the 'Prince of Peace'.

5. Who is Tiny Tim? Provide two details. (2)

Tiny Tim is Bob Cratchit's crippled son. Tiny Tim is not healthy though Bob unconvincingly tries to tell his family that Tim is growing strong and healthy. Bob is very close to Tim and dreads the thought that Tim might die in his childhood. The Ghost tells Scrooge that unless things change, the child will die.

6. Describe the third ghost. Who was he? (2)

The third ghost was the Ghost of Christmas Yet to Come. He was a "solemn phantom, draped and hooded, coming, like a mist along the ground…" He had the appearance and symbolism of the Grim Reaper. "It was shrouded in a deep black garment, which concealed its head, its face, its form, and left nothing of it visible save one outstretched hand."

7. How does Scrooge make amends, or make things right, with Bob Cratchit? (2)
Scrooge buys the big turkey that is in the store window and plans to give it to the Cratchits. He also raises Bob's salary, and assists his struggling family. Life in the office is different now as well. Scrooge and Bob talk over a bowl of soup and allows Bob to put more coal on the fire. "To Tiny Tim, he was a second father."

Paragraph Answers. Answer the following questions in a proper paragraph. (13)

1. What does the Ghost mean when he says "I see a vacant seat in the poor chimney corner, and a crutch without an owner, carefully preserved. If these shadows remain unaltered by the Future, the child will die."? (4)

The Ghost is telling Scrooge that unless the Cratchit's situation changes, Tiny Tim will die. Scrooge is being told that he would be responsible for this because of his coldness and lack of care. Scrooge scorns Bob for his meagre salary and yet it is Scrooge who pays Bob Cratchit. Scrooge has condemned the Cratchit family to a life of poverty and destitution.

2. The Ghost of Christmas Yet to Come does not speak to Scrooge, is always leading Scrooge forward, and has his hand pointed straight ahead. What does the Ghost of Christmas Yet to Come symbolize? Carefully explain. (4)

The Ghost Yet to Come symbolizes death – inevitable death. It doesn't talk, but it is always proceeding and always pointing. The tableau's that are shown in this chapter are about death and death's relentless march. Time is constantly on the move and does not wait. "Therefore never send to know for whom the bells tolls; it tolls for thee."

3. After reading *A Christmas Carol* what do you think Dickens thinks about wealth and money? Does Dickens think wealth breeds greed or is he saying something altogether different? Explain and use examples to back up your argument. (5)

Initially, Dickens's readers are led to believe that the rich are greedy and condemning and the poor, like his clerk Bob, are virtuous and good. As we read further, Dickens shows his readers that money itself is not evil, nor even the pursuit of wealth, but rather the idolization of money. Scrooge ruins all of his relationships with money – his engagement is broken off because of money, he has a strained relationship with his employee, and he has no respect for his nephew Fred. The idol of money has blinded Scrooge to see the plight around him. He, nor Marley, had no qualms about callously evicting debtors from their homes – money came first. On the other hand, we are given a glimpse of Fezziwig. Fezziwig presumably is well off and is happy and generous. He has no worries about spending money on a Christmas party and is good to Scrooge. Fred, Scrooge's nephew, seems to be well off and even offers to help Bob Cratchit out after the 'death' of Tiny Tim. Dickens does not like workhouses and debtors prisons and blames greed and love of money for these cruel and neglectful places.

<u>Bonus:</u> Who is old Scratch? <u>The Devil</u>

For Further Study...

- Have students research the Industrial Revolution. Provide primary sources of firsthand accounts of working conditions in the factories and workhouses. Have students present their finding in oral reports (i.e. PowerPoint/Prezi) or in written form. Compare the working conditions of Dickensian Britain to today in third world countries where children are still working long days in difficult circumstances.

- Have students choose a social issue of today and write their own 'parable' about it.

- Students can re-enact *A Christmas Carol*.

- Watch one of the film adaptations of *A Christmas Carol*.

- End your study of *A Christmas Carol* with a Christmas feast. Decorate the room, have the students dress in Victorian clothing, and have a potlatch lunch together.

- Pick a couple of passages out of a Christmas Carol and have a dramatic reading.

- Students can design their own dustcover for *A Christmas Carol*. The dustcover should have a cover, back page with a summary of the book, and flaps that include an 'about the author' section and some memorable quotes from the book.

Greg Slingerland is a teacher in the Niagara Region, Canada.

Made in the USA
Middletown, DE
15 December 2023

45776889R00024